THE Spooky 3D COOKBOOK

THE
Spooky
3D
COOKBOOK

hardie grant books
MELBOURNE · LONDON

CONTENTS

savoury 8

BONY DIPPERS WITH DEADLY DIP 🕷 BLOOD & GUTS PASTA
HOT POTATO CAULDRONS 🦇 BATWING NACHOS
GHOSTLY SPRING ROLLS 👻 STROPPY JOES
BAD BOY MINI PIZZAS ☠ TOXIC TORTILLA WRAPS
MONSTROUS MEATBALLS 🎃 JACK O'LANTERN MUFFINS
WITCH'S HAT SUSHI ROLLS

sweet 32

BLEEDING BERRY CRUMBLES 💀 GHOSTLY MERINGUES
EYEBALL TARTS 🎩 SEVERED FINGER COOKIES
BRAIN POPS 🧙 SCARY FAIRY BREAD
CHOCOLATE WITCHES' BREW 👻 SWAMP JELLIES
BAT COOKIES 🐈 SPIDER'S NEST CUPCAKES
POISON APPLES 🕸 CREEPY-CRAWLY FRUIT BUNS
COFFIN CAKES 🪦 SPIDER TRUFFLES

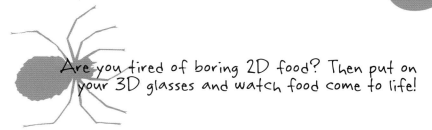

Are you tired of boring 2D food? Then put on your 3D glasses and watch food come to life!

READ THIS FIRST

Cooking 3D food is not that different from cooking 2D food: you still need to follow some basic kitchen rules. Before you begin, remember to take your 3D glasses off (no wearing them while you're chopping, using equipment or going near the stovetop!). Always ask a grown-up before you start cooking (you don't want to give them a shock when they see the mess!). Ask for help if you need to do anything tricky like chopping, handling hot pans or taking things out of the oven.

Now that we've got the safety tips out of the way, next on the list is hygiene! Wash your hands with soap before you start and try to keep your work area tidy. Keep all meat in the fridge before cooking. When you've chopped raw meat, don't use the same knife and board for other ingredients that are served uncooked, such as salad leaves or fruit.

Read the recipe ALL THE WAY TO THE END before you start cooking. You might discover ingredients or equipment you don't have (and it can be really annoying if you have to pay your younger brother or sister to run to the shop).

All the spoon measures and cup measures are LEVEL so don't use more than the recipe tells you to. One tablespoon is equal to 20 ml or 4 teaspoons. All cake and tart tins are measured across the base, not the top. We use standard 59 g (2¼ oz) eggs in the recipes, and butter is unsalted unless we say salted. If you're using the oven, arrange the shelves before you preheat the oven. A fan-forced oven will be hotter than a normal oven and doesn't need preheating. You'll need to turn your fan-forced oven 10°C (50°F) lower than the temperature in the recipe. Get a grown-up to help you with this.

When you've finished cooking, take a good look, then put on your 3D glasses and compare your dish to the picture. Magic!

SAVOURY

BONY DIPPERS WITH
deadly dip

MAKES 24 DIPPERS | **PREP TIME** 30 MINS + 1 HOUR 10 MINS RISING | **COOKING TIME** 15 MINS

125 ml (4 fl oz/$^1/_2$ cup) **lukewarm water**
1$^1/_2$ teaspoons **instant dried yeast**
1 teaspoon **caster (superfine) sugar**
1 teaspoon **salt**
250 g (9 oz/1$^2/_3$ cups) **bread (strong) flour**
1 tablespoon **olive oil**
1 teaspoon each **black olive tapenade** and **sundried tomato pesto**

DEADLY DIP
250 g (9 oz/1 cup) **sour cream** mixed with 2 tablespoons **sweet chilli sauce**

1 Combine the water, yeast, sugar and salt in a bowl. Stand for 10 minutes or until the mixture is frothy. Place the flour into a bowl and make a well in the centre. Add the yeast mixture and oil. Stir to combine. With your hands, gather the dough into a ball. Knead for 3 minutes, until smooth and elastic.

2 Divide the dough into 3 portions. Flatten out one portion of dough, and spread the tapenade onto it. Fold up the dough and knead to roughly combine (it will be squelchy). Repeat with the pesto in another portion. Place each dough into separate lightly oiled bowls, and cover with plastic wrap. Stand in a warm place for 1 hour, or until doubled in size.

3 Preheat the oven to 200°C (400°F) and oil two oven trays. Working one portion at a time, punch the dough to let out the air. Divide into 8 portions. Use your hands to roll each portion sausage about 12 cm (5 inches) long. Flatten the ends to make each sausage into a 'bone' shape. Repeat with remaining dough. Place onto the prepared trays and brush with water. Bake for 15 minutes, until lightly browned. Transfer to a wire rack to cool. Serve with the deadly dip.

BLOOD & GUTS
pasta

SERVES 4-6 | **PREP TIME** 15 MINS | **COOKING TIME** 20-25 MINS

1 tablespoon **olive oil**
1 small **onion**, chopped
500 g (1 lb 2 oz) **minced (ground) beef**
400 g (14 oz) tinned **diced tomatoes**
1 tablespoon **tomato paste (concentrated purée)**
125 ml (4 fl oz/½ cup) **salt-reduced beef stock**
1 small **eggplant (aubergine)**, chopped
1 large **zucchini (courgette)**, chopped
pinch of **sugar**
400 g (14 oz) **pasta** (in various shapes)

1 Heat the oil in a large deep frying pan over medium heat. Add the onion and cook for 5 minutes, until soft. Increase the heat to medium–high and add the minced beef. Cook for about 5 minutes, breaking up any lumps with a wooden spoon as it cooks, until browned.

2 Add the tomatoes, tomato paste and stock, and stir to combine. Add the eggplant and zucchini, and bring to the boil. Reduce the heat to low and simmer for 10–15 minutes, until the vegetables are tender. Season to taste with salt, pepper and a pinch of sugar.

3 Meanwhile, cook the pasta in a large saucepan of salted boiling water following packet directions. Drain well. Toss the pasta with the sauce, and serve.

Use a combination of unusual pasta shapes for a gross, gory effect.

HOT POTATO
cauldrons

SERVES 8 | **PREP TIME** 20 MINS | **COOKING TIME** 1 HOUR 20 MINS

8 **floury potatoes** (such as sebago), about 200 g (7 oz) each
2 teaspoons **olive oil**
3 **shortcut bacon** slices, cut into short thin strips
60 g (2 oz/$\frac{1}{2}$ cup) grated **tasty cheese**
1 small **avocado**, flesh mashed
125 g (4$\frac{1}{2}$ oz) tinned **corn kernels**, drained
2 **eggs**, separated

1 Preheat the oven to 200°C (400°F). Scrub the potatoes and prick several times with a fork. Place onto an oven tray and bake for 1 hour, or until tender when pierced with a small, sharp knife.

2 Meanwhile, heat the olive oil in a small frying pan and cook the bacon over medium heat for 3–4 minutes, until crisp. Drain on paper towels. Remove the potatoes from the oven and cool slightly. Cut off the tops and use a spoon to scoop out the flesh, leaving a 1 cm (½ inch) thick shell. Reserve half the flesh, and keep the rest for another time.

3 Mash the reserved potato flesh with a fork, and add the bacon, cheese, avocado, corn and egg yolks. Season with salt and pepper, and mix well. Beat the egg whites until stiff peaks form, and fold through the potato mixture. Spoon into the potato shells, and bake for 20 minutes, until the filling is puffed and golden brown.

BATWING
nachos

SERVES 4 | **PREP TIME** 20 MINS | **COOKING TIME** 8 MINS

125 g (4½ oz) **corn chips**
185 g (6½ oz/1½ cups) grated **cheddar cheese**
400 g (14 oz) tinned **black beans** or **red kidney beans**, rinsed and drained
125 g (4½ oz/½ cup) **mild taco sauce**
1 **avocado**, flesh mashed
125 g (4½ oz/½ cup) **sour cream**
1 tablespoon chopped **chives**
blue corn chips, to decorate

1 Preheat the oven to 180°C (350°F). Arrange the corn chips onto 4 small heatproof plates. Sprinkle with cheese. Place into the oven and cook for 5 minutes, or until the cheese melts.

2 Meanwhile, combine the beans and taco sauce in a small saucepan. Heat over medium–low heat until warmed through. Spoon into the centre of the corn chips (careful because the plates will be hot).

3 Top with a blob of mashed avocado, a dollop of sour cream and sprinkle with chives. Stand blue corn chips in the sour cream and avocado to resemble bat wings.

Look for blue corn chips in specialty food shops.

GHOSTLY
spring rolls

MAKES 20 | **PREP TIME** 30 MINS | **COOKING TIME** 0 MINS

50 g (1³/4 oz) **mung bean vermicelli (cellophane noodles)**
175 g (6 oz/1 cup) shredded **barbecued chicken**
1 large **carrot**, cut into long thin strips
1 **red capsicum (pepper)**, cut into long thin strips
1 **Lebanese (short) cucumber**, cut into long thin strips
1 small handful roughly torn **mint leaves**
20 small (16 cm/6¹/2 inch diameter) **rice-paper sheets**
sweet chilli sauce and **soy sauce**, for dipping

1 Place the noodles into a heatproof bowl and cover with boiling water. Stand for 5 minutes, then drain into a sieve. Rinse under cold running water to cool, then squeeze out the excess water. Use scissors to chop into shorter lengths.

2 Place the noodles, chicken, carrot, capsicum, cucumber and mint in a large bowl and use your hands to mix together. Soak a rice-paper sheet in a shallow dish of warm water for about 30 seconds, or until just soft. Place onto a clean cloth to absorb the excess water.

3 Place a small pile (about 3 tablespoons) of the chicken mixture in a straight line along the centre of the rice-paper sheet, leaving about 7 cm (2³/4 inches) at the bottom, with the mixture slightly overhanging at the top. Fold the bottom up over the filling, fold in the sides and roll up tightly, so some of the filling is sticking out the top. Repeat with the remaining rice-paper sheets and filling. Serve with the sauces for dipping.

Make these super scary by sticking doll arms and legs into them!

STROPPY *joes*

SERVES 6 | **PREP TIME** 15 MINS | **COOKING TIME** 15 MINS

1 tablespoon **olive oil**
1 **onion**, chopped
2 **garlic cloves**, crushed
500 g (1 lb 2 oz) **minced (ground) beef**
160 ml (5^1/2 fl oz/^{2}/3 cup) **tomato ketchup**
1 large **carrot**, shredded
80 g (3 oz/^{1}/2 cup) frozen **peas**
6 round **bread rolls**
red capsicum (pepper), **cheese slices** and **stuffed olives**, to decorate
sweet potato chips and **beetroot chips**, to serve

1 Heat the oil in a large, deep frying pan over medium heat. Add the onion and garlic and cook for 5 minutes, until soft. Increase the heat to medium–high and add the minced beef. Cook for about 5 minutes, breaking up any lumps with a wooden spoon as it cooks, until browned.

2 Stir in the tomato ketchup, carrot and peas. Reduce the heat to medium–low and cook, stirring occasionally, for 5 minutes.

3 Cut the bread rolls in half horizontally. Spoon the meat mixture over the base and replace the top at an angle. Cut 'horns' from the red capsicum, 'fangs' from the cheese slices and halve the olives to make eyes. Use toothpicks to hold in place. Serve with sweet potato and beetroot chips.

BAD BOY
mini pizzas

MAKES 12 | **PREP TIME** 30 MINS | **COOKING TIME** 10 MINS

12 individual **pizza bases** (about 12 cm/5 inch diameter)
125 ml (4¹/2 fl oz/¹/2 cup) **pizza sauce**
**cheese slices, snow peas, red capsicum (pepper), stuffed green olives,
pitted black olives, cherry tomatoes,** shredded **salami, snow pea sprouts,** to decorate

1 Preheat the oven to 180°C (350°F). You can either spread pizza sauce over each pizza base, or just put cheese on them — or pizza sauce and cheese, if you like. This gives you different coloured bases to decorate on.

2 Place the bases onto oven trays, and bake for 10 minutes, until crisp and golden brown. Cool slightly.

3 Cut angry mouth shapes from snow peas or red capsicum, and eyes from the olives. Use halved cherry tomatoes for noses, and shredded salami or snow pea sprouts for hair. Just make sure they look mean!

TOXIC
tortilla wraps

MAKES 8 | **PREP TIME** 30 MINS | **COOKING TIME** 5 MINS

1 large **avocado**
2 teaspoons **lime** or **lemon juice**
425 g (15 oz) tinned **mexe beans**
8 **tortilla wraps** (about 22 cm/8$\frac{1}{2}$ inch diameter)
150 g (5 oz) shredded **iceberg lettuce**
185 g (6$\frac{1}{2}$ oz/1$\frac{1}{2}$ cups) grated **cheddar cheese**
1 large **red capsicum (pepper)**, cut into thin strips
16 **cherry tomatoes**, quartered

1 Mash the avocado with the lime or lemon juice. Warm the mexe beans in a small saucepan or the microwave (not too hot). Lay out a wrap, and spread avocado straight down the centre.

2 Place some lettuce, cheese, capsicum, beans and tomatoes onto the wrap, in the centre third, leaving a space of about 7 cm (2$\frac{3}{4}$ inches) from the bottom and the sides.

3 Fold the lower part of the wrap up over the filling, then fold the sides over to enclose. Tie ribbon or string around the wrap to hold it in place. Repeat with the remaining wraps and filling.

Mexe beans are pinto beans in a lightly spiced sauce. You could use canned kidney beans mixed with taco sauce, if you like. For colour, use a mixture of spinach and tomato tortilla wraps.

MONSTROUS
meatballs

MAKES 15 | **PREP TIME** 30 MINS | **COOKING TIME** 10 MINS

125 g (4^{1}/$_{2}$ oz) **dried instant noodles**
500 g (1 lb 2 oz) **minced (ground) pork**
1 small **onion**, very finely chopped
2 **garlic cloves**, crushed
1 teaspoon grated **fresh ginger**
small handful roughly chopped **coriander (cilantro) leaves**
3 tablespoons **oil**
plum sauce, to serve

1 Preheat the oven to 180°C (350°F). Place the noodles into a heatproof bowl, and cover with boiling water. Stand for 2 minutes, to soften. Drain well.

2 Place the noodles into a large bowl, breaking them into shorter lengths as you do so. Add the minced pork, onion, garlic, ginger and coriander. Use your hands to mix together until evenly combined.

3 Roll 3 tablespoons of mixture into balls. Heat the oil in a large nonstick frying pan, and cook the meatballs in two batches over medium heat for 5 minutes, until browned. Gently shake the pan occasionally to turn the meatballs.

4 Transfer the meatballs to an oven tray and bake for 10 minutes, until cooked through. Serve with the plum sauce for dipping.

JACK O'LANTERN
muffins

MAKES 6 | **PREP TIME** 15 MINS | **COOKING TIME** 30 MINS

100 g (3¹/2 oz) **butter**, melted
100 g (3¹/2 oz) **bacon**, finely chopped
300 g (10¹/2 oz) grated **pumpkin (winter squash)**
225 g (8 oz/1¹/2 cups) **self-raising flour**
125 g (4¹/2 oz/1 cup) **cornmeal (cornstarch)**
large pinch of **salt**
2 **eggs**
250 ml (8¹/2 fl oz/1 cup) **milk**
90 g (3 oz/³/4 cup) grated **cheddar cheese**
parsley leaves and stalks, to decorate

1 Preheat the oven to 190°C (375°F). Spray six 170ml (6 fl oz/²/3 cup capacity) muffin holes with oil. Line the bases with small rounds of baking paper.

2 Melt the butter in a large frying pan and add the bacon. Cook over medium heat for 4–5 minutes, until lightly browned. Add the pumpkin and cook, stirring, for one more minute, until soft. Cool slightly.

3 Combine the flour, cornmeal and salt in a mixing bowl and make a well in the centre. Whisk the eggs and milk together with a fork. Add to the flour, along with the cheese and the butter, bacon and pumpkin mixture. Use a spatula to gently fold the ingredients together until just combined.

4 Spoon into the muffin holes. Bake for 25 minutes, or until risen, golden and the muffins spring back when gently touched. Leave in the tin for 5 minutes, then transfer to a wire rack. Serve warm or at room temperature. To decorate, place a parsley leaf on top of each pumpkin, and insert a stalk.

WITCH'S HAT
sushi rolls

MAKES 12 | **PREP TIME** 30 MINS | **COOKING TIME** 10 MINS + 10 MINS RESTING

110 g (4 oz/^{1}/2 cup) **sushi rice**
1 tablespoon **sushi seasoning**
3 **nori sheets**
^{1}/2 small **avocado**, flesh mashed
1 small **carrot**, shredded
10 **snow peas**, shredded
12 small **cooked prawns (shrimp)**, peeled

1 Put the rice into a sieve and rinse well under cold running water. Drain for 5 minutes. Place into a saucepan with 125 ml (4 fl oz/^{1}/2 cup) water. Cover and bring to the boil, then reduce the heat to very low and cook for 10 minutes, or until the water has been absorbed into the rice. Turn off the heat and stand, covered, for 10 minutes.

2 Transfer the rice to a large bowl. Drizzle with the sushi seasoning, and fold through with a spatula or large metal spoon. Leave to cool, turning the rice occasionally to release the heat, but don't stir too much or it will become mushy.

3 Cut the nori sheets into 4 squares. Hold a square in the palm of one hand and place 1 tablespoon of the rice diagonally across the nori. Top with a generous smear of avocado, a few strands of carrot and snow peas and a prawn.

4 Dampen one edge of the nori and roll up to form a cone shape (don't worry if it is a bit rough!). Press the damp edge to seal, dabbing with a little more water if necessary. Repeat with the remaining ingredients.

SWEET

BLEEDING
berry crumbles

MAKES 6 | **PREP TIME** 15 MINS | **COOKING TIME** 25 MINS

250 g (9 oz/2 cups) frozen **mixed berries**, thawed
400 g (14 oz) tinned **pie apple**
80 g (3 oz/$1/3$ cup) **caster (superfine) sugar**
1 teaspoon **natural vanilla extract**

TOPPING
75 g ($2^1/2$ oz/$1/2$ cup) **plain (all-purpose) flour**
50 g ($1^3/4$ oz/$1/2$ cup) **rolled (porridge) oats**
65 g ($2^1/4$ oz/$1/3$ cup) **soft brown sugar**
3 tablespoons **shredded coconut**
50 g ($1^3/4$ oz) **butter**, at room temperature, chopped

1 Preheat the oven to 180°C (350°F). Mix the berries, pie apple, sugar and vanilla together, and divide between six 185 ml (6 fl oz/$3/4$ cup) ovenproof ramekins (make sure there are berries on the top for oozing!).

2 For the topping, mix the dry ingredients together then add the butter. Use your fingertips to rub in the butter until evenly combined. Sprinkle over the berries.

3 Stand the ramekins on a baking tray. Bake for 20–25 minutes, until golden brown and the berries are oozy.

GHOSTLY
meringues

MAKES ABOUT 15 | **PREP TIME** 30 MINS | **COOKING TIME** 2 HOURS + COOLING

3 **egg whites**
170 g (6 oz/^{3}/4 cup) **caster (superfine) sugar**
1 teaspoon **white vinegar**
225 g (8 oz/1^1/2 cups) **white chocolate melts**, melted
silver and/or chocolate sprinkles, to decorate
chocolate writing icing

1 Preheat the oven to 100°C (210°F). Lightly oil two large baking trays and line with baking paper. Using electric beaters, beat the egg whites until soft peaks form. Add the sugar gradually, about 1 tablespoon at a time, beating until dissolved before you add more. Drizzle the vinegar over and beat briefly to combine.

2 Transfer most of the mixture to a large piping bag fitted with a 1.5 cm (^{5}/8 inch) plain round nozzle. Put the remaining mixture (about 3 tablespoons) into a small piping bag fitted with a 5 mm (^{1}/4 inch) nozzle. Using the large piping bag, pipe the mixture in a swirling motion onto the trays, making little ghost shapes about 4 cm (1^1/2 inches) across the base and 6 cm (2^1/4 inches) tall.

3 Using the small piping bag, pipe little arms onto each ghost (don't worry if they look wonky). Bake for 2 hours, then turn the oven off, leave the door ajar and leave to cool completely.

4 Dip the base of a ghost into the melted chocolate, about 1 cm (^{3}/8 inch) deep, and allow the excess to drain off. Dip into sprinkles, then place onto a clean sheet of baking paper to set. Repeat with the remaining ghosts. Use writing icing to makes eyes and a mouth on each ghost.

EYEBALL tarts

MAKES 12 | **PREP TIME** 20 MINS | **COOKING TIME** 10 MINS

12 frozen **mini sweet tart cases**
315 g (11 oz/1 cup) **raspberry** or **strawberry jam**
12 large **marshmallows**
12 **m&m's**
red and **black writing icing**

1 Preheat the oven to 180°C (350°F). Place the tart shells onto a baking tray, and bake for 10 minutes, until lightly golden. Set aside to cool.

2 Spoon the jam into the tart shells. Use kitchen scissors to snip the tip off each marshmallow, and place an m&m on top so they look like eyeballs. Place onto the tarts. Pipe a little black pupil onto each m&m, then pipe red veins over the marshmallows to look like bloodshot eyes.

SEVERED
finger cookies

MAKES 20 | **PREP TIME** 30 MINS | **COOKING TIME** 10–12 MINS

185 g (6¹/₂ oz) **butter**, at room temperature, chopped
170 g (6 oz/³/₄ cup) **caster (superfine) sugar**
1 teaspoon **natural vanilla extract**
300 g (10¹/₂ oz/2 cups) **plain (all-purpose) flour**
2 tablespoons **milk**
20 **blanched almonds**
strawberry or **raspberry jam**

1 Preheat the oven to 170°C (325°F). Line two baking trays with baking paper. Using electric beaters, beat the butter and sugar until light and creamy. Beat in the vanilla extract. Use a non-serrated knife to mix in the flour and milk until evenly combined. With your hands, gather the dough into a ball.

2 Take heaped tablespoons of the mixture, and shape into 'fingers' about 9 cm (3¹/₂ inches) long. Try to taper one end. Use a toothpick or flat bladed knife to press lines where the joints would be. Press an almond onto the tapered end for a fingernail.

3 Place onto the trays, and bake for 10–12 minutes, or until golden underneath (they will still be pale on top). Carefully transfer to a wire rack to cool. Serve with jam, to dip the 'severed' end of the fingers in.

BRAIN pops

MAKES ABOUT 18 | **PREP TIME** 20 MINS | **COOKING TIME** 2–3 MINS + 35 MINS SETTING

60 g (2 oz/2 cups) **rice bubbles**
65 g (2¼ oz) **butter**
90 g (3 oz/1 cup) **marshmallows**
oil, to grease
few drops **red food colouring**
150 g (5 oz/1 cup) **white chocolate melts**, melted

1 Line a large tray with baking paper. Place the rice bubbles into a large bowl and make a well in the centre. Place the butter and marshmallows into a small saucepan over low heat. Cook, stirring constantly, for 2–3 minutes or until the butter melts and the mixture is smooth.

2 Add the butter mixture to the rice bubbles and stir until well combined. Set aside for 5 minutes to cool.

3 Rub your hands with oil to prevent the mixture sticking. Take a heaped tablespoon of the mixture, and place onto a work bench. use your fingertips to shape into a ball. Transfer to the tray, and repeat with the remaining mixture. Refrigerate for 30 minutes, to set.

4 Mix a few drops of food colouring into the melted chocolate to make a fleshy pink colour. Transfer to a small piping bag fitted with a very narrow nozzle. Pipe squiggly lines over the balls. Leave for a few minutes to set. Insert a popsicle stick into each ball before serving.

SCARY
fairy bread

MAKES 12–24 PIECES | **PREP TIME** 15 MINS | **COOKING TIME** 0 MINS

12 slices fresh **white bread**
100 g (3½ oz) soft **butter**
white, brown and orange sprinkles
white chocolate writing icing
m&m's

1 Spread the bread with the butter. Use cookie cutters to cut shapes from the bread.

2 Spread the sprinkles onto separate plates. Lay a bread shape buttered-side-down onto one of the sprinkle plates and press gently so they stick.

3 If you like, pipe around the edge with writing icing (or make a spider web pattern if appropriate). Use the icing to fix m&m eyes onto the ghosts. If not serving straight away, cover with plastic wrap until serving.

Look in kitchenware shops or on line for interesting Halloween-themed cookie cutters. You can make these as large as a slice of bread, or make smaller shapes if you like, depending on the size of your cutters.

CHOCOLATE
witches' brew

MAKES 6 | **PREP TIME** 20 MINS | **COOKING TIME** 3–4 MINS + 2 HOURS CHILLING

200 g (7 oz) **dark chocolate**, chopped
2 **eggs**, separated
1 teaspoon **natural vanilla extract**
300 ml (10 fl oz) **cream**, whipped
2 x 40 g (1$\frac{1}{2}$ oz) **choc-coated peppermint bars** (or favourite chocolate bar of your choice), chopped
100 g (3$\frac{1}{2}$ oz) **chocolate cookies**, crushed
candied teeth and **plastic severed fingers**, to decorate

1 Place the chocolate into a heatproof bowl. Place over a saucepan of simmering water, making sure the base of the bowl doesn't touch the water. Stand for a few minutes, until almost melted, then stir until smooth. Leave for about 5 minutes, until cooled but still melted.

2 Stir the egg yolks and vanilla extract into the chocolate. Fold a large spoonful of the whipped cream though the chocolate mixture to help loosen it, then fold in the rest.

3 Using clean electric beaters, beat the egg whites until soft peaks form. Fold into the chocolate mixture until combined. Fold through the chopped chocolate bars. Spoon into six 185 ml (6 fl oz/$\frac{3}{4}$ cup) capacity glasses or cups, and refrigerate for about 2 hours, until set and well chilled.

4 To serve, sprinkle with crushed chocolate cookies and decorate with candy teeth, plastic severed fingers or scary toys of your choice.

SWAMP jellies

MAKES 8 | **PREP TIME** 15 MINS | **COOKING TIME** 5 MINUTES + 4½ HOURS CHILLING

1 litre (34 fl oz/4 cups) **apple juice**
2 tablespoons **powdered gelatine**
2 tablespoons **caster (superfine) sugar**
8 drops **green food colouring**
½ teaspoon **peppermint essence**
plastic critters (make it clear to your guests that these are not for eating!)
choc-coated malt balls and **green sprinkles**, to decorate

1 Place 250 ml (8½ fl oz/1 cup) of the apple juice into a microwave-safe jug. Sprinkle the gelatine over, and stand for a few minutes, until softened. Microwave on medium for 1 minute 30 seconds, then whisk to dissolve the gelatine.

2 Meanwhile, combine the remaining apple juice and the sugar in a small saucepan. Heat gently until warm, stirring to dissolve the sugar.

3 Make sure the 2 portions of juice are at about the same temperature, and mix together. Add the food colouring and peppermint essence and stir to combine. Pour half the mixture into eight 125 ml (4 fl oz/½ cup) glasses or jars. Refrigerate for 1½–2 hours, until softly set. Leave the remaining mixture in the jug at room temperature.

4 Place a plastic critter into each glass, on top of the jelly, and press in gently. Pour the remaining mixture over to fill each glass. Refrigerate for 3 hours, or until firmly set. Just before serving, crush the choc-coated malt balls, and combine with the green sprinkles. Spoon over the surface of the jellies, and decorate with more critters.

BAT Cookies

MAKES 40 | **PREP TIME** 30 MINS + 15 MINS CHILLING | **COOKING TIME** 12 MINS

250 g (9 oz) **butter**
90 g (3 oz/3/4 cup) **icing (confectioners') sugar**
2 teaspoons **natural vanilla extract**
225 g (8 oz/11/2 cups) **plain (all-purpose) flour**, sifted
150 g (5 oz/1 cup) **self-raising flour**, sifted
60 g (2 oz/1/2 cup) **unsweetened cocoa powder**, sifted
black writing icing and **small orange candies**, to decorate

1 Preheat the oven to 180°C (350°F). Line two baking trays with baking paper. Using electric beaters, beat the butter and sugar until light and creamy. Beat in the vanilla. Use a non-serrated knife to mix in the combined sifted flours and cocoa powder until the mixture clings together in small clumps.

2 Gather the dough together and turn out onto baking paper. Divide the dough in half and roll the portions out on baking paper to 7 mm (1/4 inch) thick. Place onto trays and refrigerate for 15 minutes, until firm.

3 Cut out shapes using a bat-shaped cookie cutter, about 8 cm (3 inches) wide and 4 cm (11/2 inches) high. Repeat with the other portion. Gently re-roll all the dough scraps and cut out more bats. Place onto the paper-lined trays. Bake for 12 minutes. Cool for 5 minutes on the tray, then transfer to a wire rack to cool completely.

4 Trace around the outline of each cookie, and mark lines on the wings with the writing icing. Make 2 dots for the eyes, and stick the candies onto them. Leave to set.

Look online for interesting cookie cutters if your local stores don't have them.

SPIDER'S NEST
cupcakes

MAKES 18 I **PREP TIME** 30 MINS I **COOKING TIME** 20 MINS

125 g (4^{1}/$_{2}$ oz) **butter**, at room temperature, chopped
170 g (6 oz/^{3}/4 cup) **caster (superfine) sugar**
2 teaspoons **natural vanilla extract**
2 **eggs**
2 teaspoons **red food colouring paste**
225 g (8 oz/1^{1}/2 cups) **self-raising flour**
60 g (2 oz/^{1}/2 cup) **unsweetened cocoa powder**
^{1}/2 teaspoon **bicarbonate of soda (baking soda)**
185 ml (6 fl oz/^{3}/4 cup) **buttermilk**

TOPPING
250 g (9 oz) **cream cheese**, at room temperature, chopped
185 g (6^{1}/2 oz/1^{1}/2 cups) **icing (confectioners') sugar**, sifted
1 teaspoon **natural vanilla extract**
fairy floss and **plastic spiders**, to decorate

1 Preheat the oven to 180°C (350°F). Line twelve 80 ml (3 fl oz/^{1}/3 cup) capacity muffin holes with paper cases. Using electric beaters, beat the butter, sugar and vanilla until light and creamy. Add the eggs one at a time, beating well after each addition. Add the food colouring, and beat until combined.

2 Sift the dry ingredients over the butter mixture, and add the buttermilk. Fold together until combined. Spoon into the paper cases, and bake for 20 minutes, until springy to a light touch. Cool on a wire rack.

3 For the topping, use electric beaters to beat the cream cheese until smooth. Add the sugar a little at a time, then add the vanilla extract. Spread over the cupcakes. Top with fairy floss and plastic spiders.

POISON apples

MAKES 12 | **PREP TIME** 20 MINS | **COOKING TIME** 20–25 MINS

690 g (1 lb 9 oz/3 cups) **caster (superfine) sugar**
green food colouring
12 small **apples**
sprinkles

1 Place the sugar in a large heavy-based saucepan. Add 250 ml (8 fl oz/1 cup) water, and stir over low heat, without boiling, until the sugar has dissolved.

2 Increase the heat to medium–high and bring to the boil. Clip a candy thermometer onto the side of the pan, in the liquid. Cook, without stirring, for 20–25 minutes, until the temperature reaches 150°C (300°F), which is called the 'hard crack stage'. If you don't have a candy thermometer, drop a small spoonful of the mixture into a cup of cold water. If it sets hard instead of being pliable, it is ready.

3 Meanwhile, insert clean sticks or thick wooden skewers (even chopstick are good!) into the apples. Line a large, heatproof tray with baking paper. Remove the pan from the heat and allow the bubbles to subside. Add about 6 drops of food colouring, and swirl very briefly with a wooden spoon. Spread sprinkles onto separate saucers.

4 Dip an apple into the toffee. Tilt the pan slightly and turn the apple to coat evenly. Let the excess drip back into the pan, and dip into the sprinkles. Place onto the tray and leave for 20 minutes, to set hard. Repeat with other apples.

Take great care handling toffee and sugar syrup – this is a job that requires adult supervision!

CREEPY-CRAWLY
fruit buns

MAKES 12 | **PREP TIME** 30 MINS + 1 HOUR 20 MINS RISING | **COOKING TIME** 20 MINS

330 ml (11 fl oz/1¹/3 cups) **warm milk**
2 teaspoons **instant dried yeast**
2 tablespoons **caster (superfine) sugar**
525 g (1 lb 2 oz/3¹/2 cups) **plain (all-purpose) flour**
60 g (2 oz) **butter**, melted
90 g (3 oz/³/4 cup) **sultanas (golden raisins)**
450 g (1 lb) tub **chocolate frosting**
white and dark chocolate sprinkles

1 Whisk the milk, yeast and 1 teaspoon of the sugar together. Set aside for 5 minutes, until frothy. Combine the flour and remaining sugar in a bowl, and make a well in the centre.

2 Add the milk mixture and butter to the well. Use a wooden spoon to combine the mixture until it is evenly moistened. With your hands, gather the dough into a ball. Turn out onto a lightly floured work surface and knead for 5 minutes, until smooth. Flatten out the dough, and sprinkle the sultanas over. Fold up and knead for another 2 minutes, until evenly combined.

3 Place into a lightly oiled bowl, cover loosely with plastic wrap and set aside in a warm place for 1 hour, until doubled in size.

4 Punch the dough to expel the air, and knead again until smooth. Divide the dough into 12 portions, and roll each out to a 'sausage' 12 cm (5 inches) long. Arrange on two trays lined with baking paper, leaving space between each one. Cover loosely with plastic wrap and set aside for 20 minutes, to rise. Preheat the oven to 180°C (350°F). Bake for 20 minutes, until golden brown and cooked through. Transfer to a wire rack to cool. Spread frosting onto the buns, and decorate with the white and dark chocolate sprinkles.

COFFIN cakes

SERVES 12–16 | **PREP TIME** 30 MINS | **COOKING TIME** 30 MINS

250 g (9 oz) **butter**, chopped
250 g (9 oz) **dark chocolate**, chopped
3 **eggs**
200 g (7 oz/1 cup) **soft brown sugar**
1 teaspoon **natural vanilla extract**
110 g (4 oz/³/4 cup) **plain (all-purpose) flour**
3 tablespoons **self-raising flour**
250 g (9 oz) **white fondant icing**
2 tablespoons **unsweetened cocoa powder**

1 Preheat the oven to 170°C (325°F). Grease a 20 x 30 cm (8 x 12 inch) slab tin and line with baking paper, extending over the two long sides.

2 Place the butter and chocolate into a heatproof bowl, and sit over a saucepan of simmering water (make sure the bottom of the bowl doesn't touch the water). Stir over low heat until melted and smooth. Cool slightly.

3 In another bowl, use electric beaters to beat the eggs, sugar and vanilla for 3 minutes, until pale and frothy. Add the chocolate mixture and beat briefly to combine. Sift the flours over and fold in until just combined. Pour into the prepared tin, and bake for 30 minutes. Leave in the pan to cool to room temperature, then refrigerate overnight, until firm.

4 Lift out of the tin, and cut into 4 large rectangles. Trim to make coffin shapes (the cook gets to eat the trimmings!). Press out the fondant icing to about 2 cm (³/4 inch) thick. Place the cocoa powder into a small bowl, and add ¹/2–1 teaspoon of water, to make a thick paste. Dot over the fondant icing, and knead roughly until partially combined and slightly marbled. Dust a workbench with icing sugar, and roll out the fondant until about 3 mm (¹/8 inch) thick. Cut out coffin shapes the same size as the cakes, and place on top.

SPIDER truffles

MAKES 4 | **PREP TIME** 30 MINS + 30 MINS CHILLING | **COOKING TIME** 2–3 MINS

250 g (9 oz) **plain cookies**
40 g (1½ oz/⅓ cup) **unsweetened cocoa powder**
90 g (3 oz/1 cup) **desiccated (grated dried) coconut**
400 g (14 oz) tinned **condensed milk**
30 g (1 oz) **butter**, melted
55 g (2 oz/1 cup) **shredded coconut**
black food colouring
writing icing and **pipe cleaners**, to decorate

1 Put the cookies into a plastic bag and hit with a rolling pin until crushed into small pieces. Transfer to a bowl. Add the cocoa powder and desiccated coconut. Make a well in the centre. Add the condensed milk and melted butter. Mix together with a wooden spoon until evenly moistened. Chill for 30 minutes.

2 Place half the shredded coconut into a plastic bag and add a few drops of food colouring. Gently press the air out of the bag, and hold the end closed. Rub the outside of the bag to roughly mix the colour through. Transfer to a plate.

3 Dry fry the remaining coconut over medium heat for 2–3 minutes, stirring often, until golden. Transfer to a plate and leave to cool.

4 Roll slightly heaped tablespoons of the mixture into balls then flatten the bases. Roll in the coconut. Keep in an airtight container in the fridge. Press black shredded coconut over half the truffles, and toasted coconut over the remaining truffles. Trim pipe cleaners and insert to make legs, and pipe eyes and a stripe onto the bodies.

 INDEX

A

apples, poison **54**

B

bad boy mini pizzas **23**
bat cookies **50**
batwing nachos **16**
bleeding berry crumbles **34**
blood & guts pasta **12**
bony dippers with deadly
    dip **11**
brain pops **42**
buns, creepy-crawly fruit **57**

C

cakes
    coffin cakes **58**
    spider's nest cupcakes **53**
chocolate witches' brew **46**
coffin cakes **58**
cookies
    bat cookies **50**
    severed finger cookies **41**
creepy-crawly fruit buns **57**
cupcakes, spider's nest **53**

D

dip, deadly **11**

E

eyeball tarts **38**

F

fairy bread, scary **45**

G

ghostly meringues **37**
ghostly spring rolls **19**

H

hot potato cauldrons **15**

J

jack o'lantern muffins **28**
jellies, swamp **49**

M

meatballs, monstrous **27**
meringues, ghostly **37**
monstrous meatballs **27**
muffins, jack o'lantern **28**

N

nachos, batwing **16**

P

pasta, blood & guts **12**
pizzas, bad boy mini **23**
poison apples **54**
potato, hot cauldrons **15**

S

scary fairy bread **45**
severed finger cookies **41**
spider truffles **61**
spider's nest cupcakes **53**
spring rolls, ghostly **19**
stroppy joes **20**
sushi rolls, witch's hat **31**
swamp jellies **49**

T

tarts, eyeball **38**
toxic tortilla wraps **24**
truffles, spider **61**

W

witch's hat sushi rolls **31**

Published in 2012 by Hardie Grant Books

Hardie Grant Books (Australia)
Ground Floor, Building 1
658 Church Street
Richmond, Victoria 3121
www.hardiegrant.com.au

Hardie Grant Books (UK)
Second Floor, North Suite
Dudley House, Southampton Street
London WC2E 7HF
www.hardiegrant.co.uk

Publishing director: Paul McNally
Design manager: Heather Menzies
Original design concept: Lauren Camilleri
3D imaging: Ben Hutchings
Photographer: Benito Martin
Stylist: Jane Collins
Recipe writing: Tracy Rutherford
Production manager: Penny Sanderson

Cataloguing-in-Publication data is available from the National Library
of Australia.

ISBN 9781742703176

Colour reproduction by Splitting Image Colour Studio
Printed in China by 1010 Printing International Limited